© 2022/1444 by Ihya Publishing

All rights reserved. No part of this publication may be reproduced, distributed, or transmitted in any form or by any means, including photocopying, recording, or other electronic or mechanical methods, without the prior written permission of the Ihya Publishing the Publisher.

Printed in Türkiye by Mega Printing

First Printing, 2022

ISBN 978-1-939256-10-2 (Hardcover)

Published by:
Ihya Publishing
P.O. Box 426
Alburtis, PA-18011
www.ihyapublishing.com
info@ihyapublishing.com

Author	Nelly Elmenshawy
Illustrations	Uzma Ahmad
Cover Design & Book Design by	Uzma Ahmad

Distributed by
Muslim Publishers Group
www.mpgbooks.com
info@mpgbooks.com
+1 (844) 674-2665

Ihya Publishing is a non-profit 501(c)(3) publishing house.

SUN & MOON

A Conversation About God

Nelly Elmenshawy
Illustrated by Uzma Ahmad

**A message to
the reader:**

Please be kind to this book
and keep it in a special place.
This story is about God,
written out of love for the
knowledge of God.

Dedication

In memory of my beloved parents,
may God have mercy on them.

Long, long ago, in a faraway place, there were two very good friends and their names were Sun and Moon. They were the closest of companions and often talked about the most important of matters.

Moon loved to talk with Sun because Sun was much brighter than him.

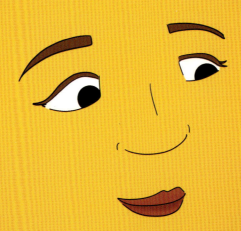
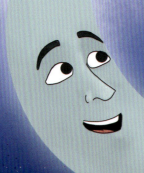

One day, Sun and Moon were having a very special conversation. They talked about many things, but on that day, Moon wanted to know something very special and very important.

"Sun."

"Yes, Moon."

"Can you tell me about God?"

"Why yes, I would love to tell you about God," Sun said. "This is my favorite topic! You see, it has always been so. There has always been God. He has always been alive, even before you and I were created."

"Really? Please tell me more!" Moon said.

Moon listened very carefully as Sun began to speak. "There was a time when there was nothing in creation. Even you and I weren't here.

God wanted us to know Him, so He created everything that you see in the heavens and the earth, like the mountains, forests, fields, rivers and oceans.

And then God created Adam, and from Adam came the souls of all the other humans. Among the souls was the Best of Creation, the most beloved to God: Prophet Muhammad, peace be upon him."

"Of course! The Beloved, peace be upon him," Moon exclaimed.

"One day God brought all of the souls together- the souls of all these people living on Earth, those of the past, and those still to come. He asked them a very important question."

"What could that question be?" asked a puzzled Moon. "If God created them, shouldn't He have all the answers?"

"Moon, you are so smart," said Sun, quite
pleased with Moon's cleverness. "Yes,
of course, God has ALL of the answers to
ALL of the questions. God knows everything!
Yet, He wanted the souls to remember
this moment, one that would be
imprinted in the heart of every
soul forever." Moon listened
very closely as
Sun continued.

"God asked all of the souls, 'Am I not your Lord?'"

"How did God speak to them?" Moon asked.

"God's Speech is not words or sounds. It is not like ours, Moon. He is not like anything in creation. But His Speech is perfect; you know, everything about God is perfect."

"Oh," Moon replied, wanting to know more. "What did the souls say?"

"The souls answered, 'Yes, we bear witness.' They knew who their Lord was.

In fact, the souls always knew the truth about God, even before they answered His question. They always knew their Creator because He placed that knowledge in them. Souls do not forget God and God never forgets them. So, you see Moon, it has always been that God exists and that He knows everything, sees everything and hears everything."

Moon thought for a moment and whispered, "Can God hear us now?"

"Yes, and He already knows how this very moment- and every moment- will be." Sun said, reassuring her friend.

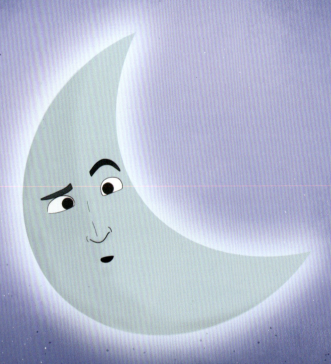

"How is that? Is that even possible?"

Upon seeing Moon a bit confused, Sun simply said, "Anything is possible for God. Remember that He is not like any of His creation. There is nothing like Him, and He is One."

Moon thanked Sun for their very special conversation. He had learned so much that day.

After some time had passed, Sun noticed that Moon was shining a little brighter in the distance.

"Oh Sun! Today I listened to the singing of the birds. It was breathtaking! They were praising God with song."

Sun could see Moon's excitement.
Moon seemed to be changing.
He was seeing things more clearly now.

Moon continued to watch the birds for some time when he had another very important question.

"I have been thinking. I have been watching the birds. They change. Some seem young but some are older. They do not always come back. Where do they go?"

"What an excellent question!" Sun said. "Like all of creation, birds too have a beginning and an end. Just as you and I had a beginning, one day we will no longer shine in the sky."

"Where will we go?" Moon became uneasy.

"Only God knows, but I am sure it will be perfect," Sun gently reassured her friend.

"Will God die with us?"

"Oh no, Moon! God has complete life. Remember that He has always been in existence, and He will always exist, forever. God does not die."

For a long while, Moon remained quiet.

"Moon, why have you been so quiet?" Sun asked.

"I have been thinking about God. I have been wondering . . ."

"Ahem. Excuse me."

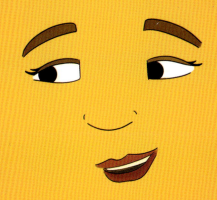

Sun and Moon looked up and found that they had a visitor. It was their old friend Earth.

"I have been listening to the both of you for a long time," Earth said. "I too want to join in this very special conversation."

"Welcome! Welcome! We would love to have you join us. Wouldn't we, Moon?"

"Why yes, of course!" Moon replied. "Tell us, Earth, what do you have to share with us?"

Earth began, "I have witnessed so many amazing events during my lifetime.
I have witnessed Kun fa-yakūn."

Moon said nothing.
He was very confused.
And this time,
even Sun was
speechless.

They did not know what 'Kun fa-yakūn' meant.

Earth continued, "I have witnessed 'Be! And it is'."

Sun and Moon remained silent, they needed more explanation.

"I have witnessed creation happening. I have seen flowers bloom, babies born, rain fall, and waves crash! God does all of this by Himself without help from anyone!

This happens by God having complete and perfect Knowledge, Will, and Power. He knows of a matter, He Wills it to happen, and He has the Power to make it happen!"

At first, Sun and Moon stared at each other in silence. Then suddenly, Moon's eyes widened. He shone very bright in the sky- so bright that for a moment you could not tell which was Sun and which was Moon!

Moon could not contain his excitement!

"KUN FA-YAKŪN! BE! AND IT IS!

I have witnessed so many amazing events! We all have. We are witnessing it now! Oh, this is grand! The grandest of grand and the bestest of best!"

Suddenly, Sun began to beam!
She also understood what
Earth had said.

Sun, Moon and Earth were so happy. They rejoiced in their knowledge of God. They became the best of friends. Over time, they had many more special conversations, and they learned more and more about God and His creation. They understood that God is perfect and everything He does is perfect.

"Isn't it all amazing?" Moon asked Sun one day.

"It is," sighed Sun. "Everything about our Creator is wondrous. Subhan Allah."